SCIENCE WORKSHOP

ELEMENTS · MIXTURES AND REACTIONS

Mick Seller

SHOOTING STAR PRESS®

This edition produced in 1995 for
Shooting Star Press Inc
230 Fifth Avenue
Suite 1212
New York, NY 10001

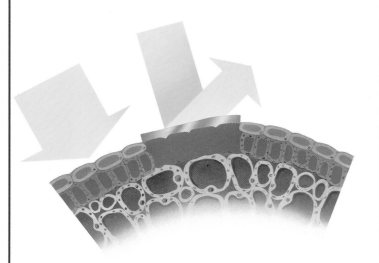

Created and designed by
N. W. Books
28 Percy Street
London W1P 0LD

Design	David West
	Children's Book
Designer	Keith Newell
Editors	Suzanne Melia
	Richard Green
Picture Researcher	Emma Krikler
Illustrator	Ian Thompson
Consultant	Bryson Gore

First published in
the United States in 1995 by
Shooting Star Press Inc

ISBN 1-57335-328-0

CONTENTS

PHOTOCREDITS

All the photographs in this book are by Roger Vlitos apart from pages; 8 top left, 22 top, 24 top: Science Photo Library; 10 top: Eye Ubiquitous; 12 top, 26 top: Frank Spooner Pictures.

INTRODUCTION

The world which we see around us – our friends, trees, houses, cars, in fact everything – is built up from the 105 simple substances called elements. Some elements exist in a pure form on their own, such as the particles of oxygen in the air that we breathe or the copper from which most of our water pipes are made; some combine with other elements to build simple compounds, such as hydrogen and oxygen, to make water; and others combine in more complex ways, sugar for example, is a compound of carbon, hydrogen and oxygen. The smallest piece of any element, almost too small to be seen with even the most powerful microscope, is called an atom. When different atoms join together during reactions they form particles, or molecules, of new substances. Everyday, we are surrounded by hundreds of reactions without which our lives would grind to a halt. Therefore, by learning about the subject of elements and reactions we can begin to understand the world around us and how it works.

Why It Works explaining
science ideas

Introduction

Bright Ideas
for further
projects

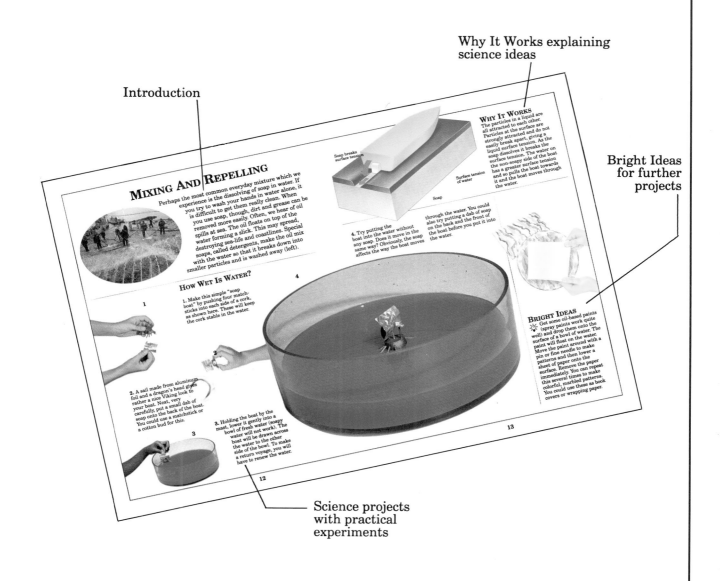

MIXING AND REPELLING

Perhaps the most common everyday mixture which we experience is the dissolving of soap in water. If you try to wash your hands in water alone, it is difficult to get them really clean. When you use soap, though, dirt and grease can be removed more easily. Often, we hear of oil spills at sea. The oil floats on top of the water forming a slick. This may spread, destroying sea-life and coastlines. Special soaps, called detergents, make the oil mix with the water so that it breaks down into smaller particles and is washed away (left).

HOW WET IS WATER?

1. Make this simple "soap boat" by pushing four matchsticks into each side of a cork, as shown here. These will keep the cork stable in the water.

2. A sail made from aluminum foil and a dragon's head gives your boat a nice Viking look to rather a boat. Next, very carefully, put a small dab of soap onto the back of the boat. You could use a matchstick or a cotton bud for this.

3. Holding the boat by the mast, lower it gently into a bowl of fresh water (soapy water will not work). The boat will be drawn across the water to the other side of the bowl. To make a return voyage, you will have to renew the water.

4. Try putting the boat into the water without any soap. Does it move in the same way? Obviously, the soap affects the way the boat moves through the water. You could also try putting a dab of soap on the back and the front of the boat before you put it into the water.

WHY IT WORKS

The particles in a liquid are all attracted to each other. Particles at the surface are strongly attracted and do not easily break apart, giving a liquid surface tension. As the soap dissolves it breaks the surface tension. The water on the non-soapy side of the boat has a greater surface tension and so pulls the boat towards it and the boat moves through the water.

Soap breaks
surface tension

Surface tension
of water

Soap

BRIGHT IDEAS

Get some oil-based paints (spray paints work quite well) and drop them onto the surface of a bowl of water. The paint will float on the water. Move the paint around with a pin or fine needle to make patterns and then lower a sheet of paper onto the surface. Remove the paper immediately. You can repeat this several times to make colorful, marbled patterns. You could use these as book covers or wrapping paper.

Science projects
with practical
experiments

THE WORKSHOP

A science workshop is a place to test ideas, perform experiments and make discoveries. To prove many scientific facts you don't need a lot of fancy equipment. In fact, everything you need for a basic workshop can be found around your home or school. Read through these pages and then use your imagination to add to your "home laboratory". As you work your way through this book, you should enjoy completing the projects and seeing the ideas work. Remember, though, that from a scientific point of view the projects are just the starting point. For example, when you finish the "soap boat" project on pages 12 and 13, experiment to see whether other substances work in the same way as the soap. You could try butter, dish washing liquid and so on. Do be careful though. Never take any substances without the permission of an adult. Many household chemicals are deadly poisonous. Also, by sharing ideas you will learn more.

MAKING MODELS

When making models and carrying out tests and experiments read through all the steps before you begin. Then make a list of the things you need and collect them together. Next, think about the project so that you have a clear idea of what you are about to do. Finally, take your time putting models together and carrying out tests. If something goes wrong, retrace your steps. And if you can't fix it, start over again. Every scientist makes mistakes but the best ones never give up.

GENERAL TIPS

There are at least two parts to every experiment; experimenting with materials and testing a scientific fact. If you don't have the exact materials for the projects in this book you must be patient and wait until you have had a chance to collect the correct substances and equipment. Once you've finished experimenting, read your notes thoroughly and think about what happened. Always try to draw conclusions, even if the project went wrong.

SAFETY WARNINGS

Make sure that an adult knows what you are doing at all times. When cooking, always make sure that equipment, work surfaces and your hands are clean. All forms of heating can be dangerous. Therefore, only use candles, ovens or irons if you have an adult to help. Never taste or smell the substances that you are working with.

Always conduct a "fair test". Change one thing at a time for each stage of an experiment, then you can always tell which change caused a different result. As you go along, record what you see. Ask questions, such as "how?", "why?" and "what if ?". Carry out your test and make notes about what happens. Compare your results to those of your friends and classmates.

WHAT ARE ELEMENTS?

Everything in the world is made up of elements. An element is a simple chemical substance which itself is made of tiny particles called atoms. Diamonds (right) are made from the element, carbon. There are 105 elements known to man. Some, like iron or copper, were used in ancient times, while others have been made by modern scientists. Many elements can be combined to make new substances – copper and tin can be melted together to make an alloy (mixture) called bronze. The periodic table arranges all the known elements in a special way.

PERIODIC TABLE

1. Each square contains the symbol for a different element. The symbol comes from the common name or Latin name of the element; C stands for carbon and Al for aluminum. The Latin for iron is ferrum, so the symbol is Fe.

H								
Li	Be							
Na	Mg							
K	Ca	SC	Ti	V	Cr	Mn	Fe	C
Rb	Sr	Y	Zr	Nb	Mo	Tc	Ru	F
Cs	Ba	La	Hf	Ta	W	Re	Os	
Fr	Ra	Ac						

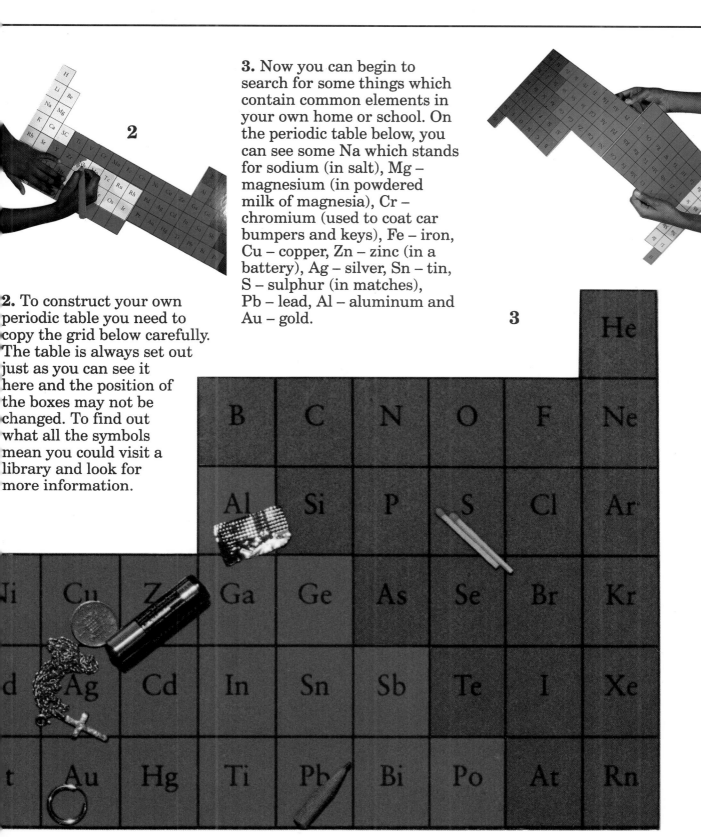

2

2. To construct your own periodic table you need to copy the grid below carefully. The table is always set out just as you can see it here and the position of the boxes may not be changed. To find out what all the symbols mean you could visit a library and look for more information.

3. Now you can begin to search for some things which contain common elements in your own home or school. On the periodic table below, you can see some Na which stands for sodium (in salt), Mg – magnesium (in powdered milk of magnesia), Cr – chromium (used to coat car bumpers and keys), Fe – iron, Cu – copper, Zn – zinc (in a battery), Ag – silver, Sn – tin, S – sulphur (in matches), Pb – lead, Al – aluminum and Au – gold.

3

Now try to find some... C – carbon (soot, pencil lead, diamonds and charcoal are all forms of carbon), Hg – mercury (the silver stuff in thermometers), Pt – platinum (a metal used in jewelry making) and Cl – chlorine (added to drinking water to kill bacteria).

STATES OF MATTER

Elements can be found in 3 forms or "states"; solid, liquid or gas. It is possible to change the state of elements; for example, by heating iron in a furnace (left) it can be melted, changing from a solid to a liquid. Oxygen, the gas which is so important for all forms of life, can be cooled down to a point where it becomes liquid. Sometimes elements join together to form new substances, known as compounds – water is a compound made from hydrogen and oxygen. Compounds, like elements, can exist in different states. Water can be a solid (ice), a liquid or it can be almost like a gas (steam).

WHY IT WORKS

If you could see the molecules (small particles) in a substance, you would notice that they seem to quiver. In a solid like ice, though, they are tightly bound and cannot move far (1). When ice is heated, the molecules quiver faster. At the point when the ice melts, they move away from their fixed place and start to slide around. The molecules are more spaced out in the liquid (2). As water is heated, the molecules move faster still and break away from each other, moving freely in the air (3). The whole process is reversed when we stop heating the water and start to cool it down.

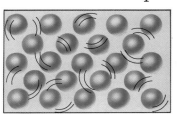

1

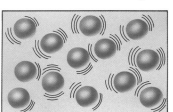

2

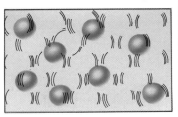

3

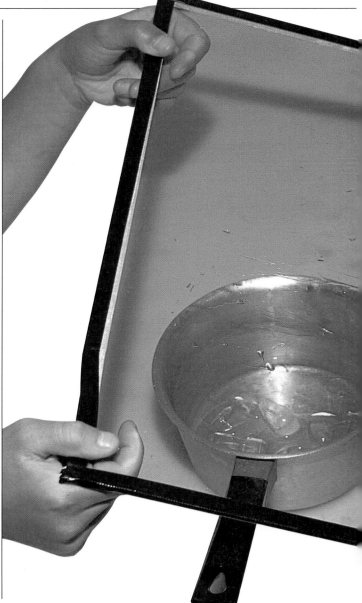

MOLECULES IN MOTION

1. We can watch the changes of state in this simple experiment with water. Empty a tray of ice-cubes into a saucepan. Put them on the stove on a low heat so that they melt slowly. You are changing a solid to a liquid.

1

2. After a while the liquid becomes hot and turns to steam. Put the ice-cube tray into a metal bowl or pan and place this next to your saucepan. Place a metal tray over the saucepan, as shown here, to catch the steam. (We've used glass here so that you can see underneath.)

2

BRIGHT IDEAS

 Scientists often make models in order to show what is happening in experiments like this. You can have a go at this too. Find a small tin or box, or make a small cube from card. Next, you'll need a lid from a shoe box or something similar and a large tray which has sides. Into each, place about 25 marbles. The marbles represent the molecules of water. Now you need to make your molecules quiver just as real molecules of water do. Place the three containers on a table or a bed and shake it gently. You'll see the marbles in the cube will move only a little (like the molecules in a solid), those in the lid are more active (liquid), and the ones on the tray move around very freely (like a gas).

3. As the steam hits the tray it cools down and changes back to a liquid. Once you have collected the liquid in the ice-cube tray you can return the tray to the freezer.

3

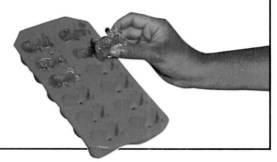

4. After a few hours, you'll be able to remove the ice-cubes from the freezer. The changes of state have now gone full circle – solid to liquid to gas to liquid and back to solid again.

4

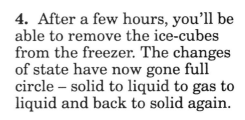

SPLITTING MIXTURES

To form a new compound, the atoms of different elements must join to each other; for example, in damp conditions oxygen combines with iron to make rust. Rust, or iron oxide, is a new compound which has resulted from a chemical reaction between the atoms of iron and oxygen. It is very difficult to remove the oxygen and convert the rust back to iron. In mixtures, no chemical reaction takes place and it is possible to get the original elements back more easily. Salt can be obtained from the sea by evaporating the water away (left).

WHY IT WORKS

Most colors in ink pens or paints are not pure colors but rather mixtures of several colors. Some colors in each mixture cling strongly to the paper, while others cling less and so move through the paper more quickly. As the individual colors move at different rates they are separated out from the original mixture, and because each mixture is slightly different to start with, each strip of paper, or chromatogram, is slightly different too.

Black

Secondary colors

Primary colors

INK-DOT DETECTIVE

1. Use three different black felt-pens and three strips of blotting paper. Draw a symbol on one end of each strip and identify each piece and the pen used with a colored dot.

1

2. Now fill a large bowl with water. It should be large enough to dangle the three pieces of paper into the water at the same time.

2

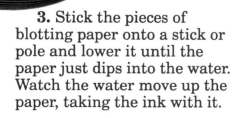

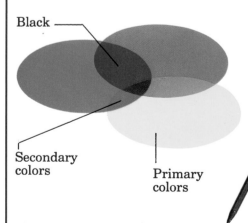

3. Stick the pieces of blotting paper onto a stick or pole and lower it until the paper just dips into the water. Watch the water move up the paper, taking the ink with it.

BRIGHT IDEAS

Mix some iron filings up with powdered limestone. You'll see that the color of the mixture is different to the color of the substances you started with; the dark grey and white have combined to make a light grey. No chemical change has taken place, however, and what you have made is not a new compound, but a mixture.

With the use of a strong magnet it is quite easy to remove the iron filings so that once again you have two pure substances.

Iron filings

Magnet

Powdered limestone

4. Look at each of the pieces of blotting paper. The black marks should have split up into separate colors. Remember which color band goes with which pen.

4

5. Give the pens to three friends and look away while one of them marks a piece of blotting paper. Dip the paper in the water and by looking at the band of colors you will know whose pen made the mark.

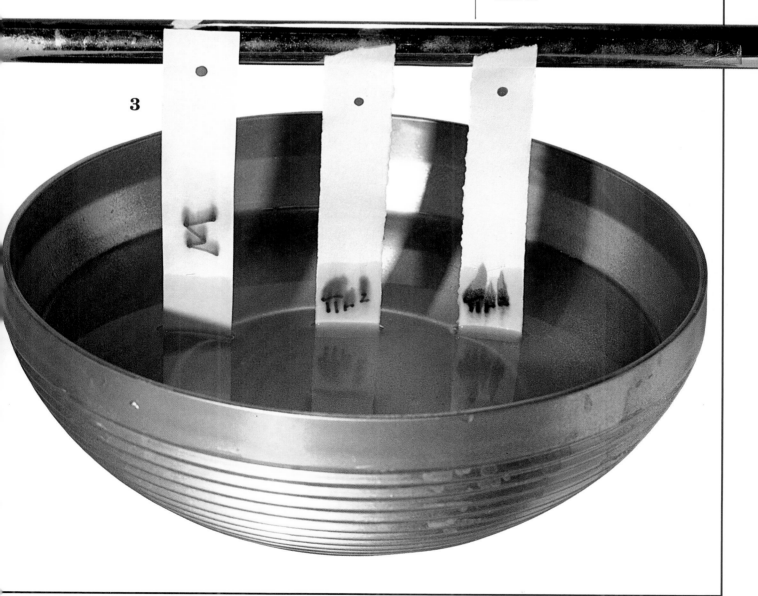

3

MIXING AND REPELLING

Perhaps the most common everyday mixture which we experience is the dissolving of soap in water. If you try to wash your hands in water alone, it is difficult to get them really clean. When you use soap, though, dirt and grease can be removed more easily. Often, we hear of oil spills at sea. The oil floats on top of the water forming a slick. This may spread, destroying sea-life and coastlines. Special soaps, called detergents, make the oil mix with the water so that it breaks down into smaller particles and is washed away (left).

HOW WET IS WATER?

1

1. Make this simple "soap boat" by pushing four matchsticks into each side of a cork, as shown here. These will keep the cork stable in the water.

4

2

2. A sail made from aluminum foil and a dragon's head gives rather a nice Viking look to your boat. Next, very carefully, put a small dab of soap onto the back of the boat. You could use a matchstick or a cotton bud for this.

3

3. Holding the boat by the mast, lower it gently into a bowl of fresh water (soapy water will not work). The boat will be drawn across the water to the other side of the bowl. To make a return voyage, you will have to renew the water.

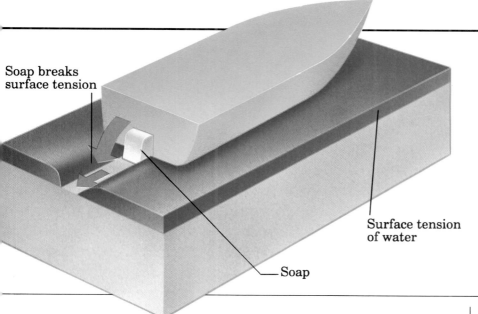

Soap breaks surface tension

Surface tension of water

Soap

WHY IT WORKS

The particles in a liquid are all attracted to each other. Particles at the surface are strongly attracted and do not easily break apart, giving a liquid surface tension. As the soap dissolves it breaks the surface tension. The water on the non-soapy side of the boat has a greater surface tension and so pulls the boat towards it and the boat moves through the water.

4. Try putting the boat into the water without any soap. Does it move in the same way? Obviously, the soap affects the way the boat moves through the water. You could also try putting a dab of soap on the back and the front of the boat before you put it into the water.

BRIGHT IDEAS

Get some oil-based paints (spray paints work quite well) and drop them onto the surface of a bowl of water. The paint will float on the water. Move the paint around with a pin or fine needle to make patterns and then lower a sheet of paper onto the surface. Remove the paper immediately. You can repeat this several times to make colorful, marbled patterns. You could use these as book covers or wrapping paper.

13

VISIBLE REACTIONS

Have you ever wondered why cakes rise in the oven or what the bubbles in soda are actually made of ? The answer in each case is the same – carbon dioxide. Carbon dioxide is a gas which is formed when two atoms of oxygen join with one atom of carbon. The formula for carbon dioxide is CO_2. There are actually small amounts of carbon dioxide in the air and green plants give out CO_2 during the hours of darkness. The CO_2 in cakes, however, is not drawn from the air. It is produced when acids react with carbonates or bicarbonates which are present in the ingredients.

VOLCANIC ERUPTION

1. Make a volcano which erupts with a foam of vinegar and baking powder. Form a cone shape around an old plastic cup or bowl. Glue the cone firmly to a base.

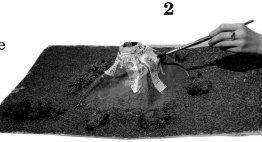

2. Cover the cone with 5 or 6 layers of newspaper and glue and leave to dry. Next, cover the base with glue and sprinkle with sawdust or sand. Paint the base and volcano.

3. When dry, a coat of sealing mixture (3 parts water to 1 part glue) will help to protect the paintwork when the volcano erupts. Once again, allow the whole thing to dry well before the next step.

4. Next, prepare the ingredients which will produce the reaction. You will need a small amount of baking powder or bicarbonate of soda and some vinegar mixed with a little red food-coloring.

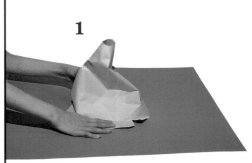

5. Put a teaspoon of the baking powder into the volcano then pour in a little vinegar. The reaction should be fast and a red liquid containing carbon dioxide will foam up over the sides of your volcano as it "erupts".

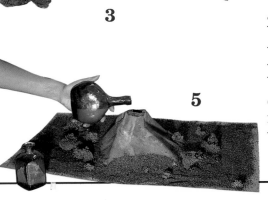

WHY IT WORKS

The vinegar is an acid and it reacts with the sodium bicarbonate (which is an alkali) in the baking powder. This reaction produces carbon dioxide gas. If you add water to baking powder you would also get a reaction, although it would be a slower one. This is because the baking powder contains acidic salts which become acids when the water is added. These acids react with the sodium bicarbonate to produce CO_2. It is partly this reaction which causes cakes to rise in the oven.

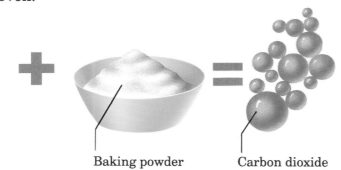

Vinegar   Baking powder   Carbon dioxide

BRIGHT IDEAS

Why not make your own fizzing lemonade? Mix the juice of 4 lemons with 1 quart of water then add sugar until your mixture tastes good. When you want a drink, pour out a glass, add half a teaspoon of bicarbonate of soda, stir and drink at once!

6. Obviously, the more ingredients you use, the bigger the size of the eruption. A fizzing noise, known as effervescence, can be heard – this is the sound of the carbon dioxide gas being produced.

6

MAKING NEW MATERIALS

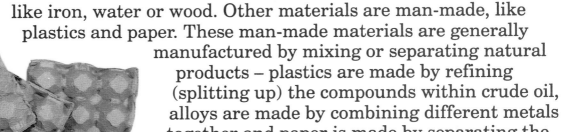

Many of the materials that we use are naturally occurring elements or compounds, like iron, water or wood. Other materials are man-made, like plastics and paper. These man-made materials are generally manufactured by mixing or separating natural products – plastics are made by refining (splitting up) the compounds within crude oil, alloys are made by combining different metals together and paper is made by separating the fibers from trees and processing them to make paper. The egg carton (left), cardboard boxes, blotting paper, the book you are reading now, all these things started out life as trees!

PAPER MASK

1

1. You can recycle old newspaper to make a new material called papier mâché. Mix up a thin paste of flour and water. Then, cover a balloon with a thin coat of oil.

3

4. Cut out the features of your mask. This can be a bit difficult so you could ask an adult to begin. Next, paint the mask, making sure your paint is not too wet.

5

6. If you want, you could now recycle the mask itself. Soaking in water will reverse the papier mâché process and turn the mask back to newspaper and paste.

2. Tear up strips of newspaper, dip them in the paste and cover the balloon with 5 or 6 layers. Leave to dry until the paper is very hard.

2

3. Carefully cut the papier mâché away from the balloon. You'll find that the coating of oil will stop it sticking to the balloon too badly. Cut the shape in half.

4

5. Your mask is an example of recycling, that is, taking an old material which you no longer need and putting it to a new use.

6

WHY IT WORKS

Papier mâché is formed by layers of paper which are bonded together with adhesive paste. The flour (1) is made into a paste by adding water (2). This paste is then added to the paper (3) and soaks into the pores. As the water evaporates away (4), the molecules are pulled tighter together and the bond becomes solid.

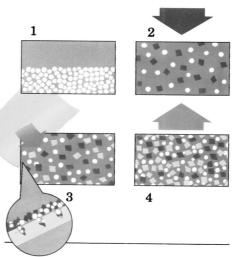

BRIGHT IDEAS

The clay and straw bricks in very old houses are made in the same way as papier mâché. Can you think of any more materials made this way?

A clay and straw brick

REACTIONS AND HEAT

To get a chemical reaction started, some form of energy is usually needed. This may simply be heat energy taken from the warmth of a room, or it may be the energy which is taken from a blast furnace where iron is taken from iron ore. Many things which we rely on have to be heated before they are ready for use. Think of a cup made of clay which has never been baked in a kiln, bricks which are still soft clay or a loaf of bread left as raw dough. Without reactions started by high levels of heat these things are not quite the same. Even the coffee that we drink gets its rich flavor when the beans are roasted (left).

DOUGH JEWELRY

1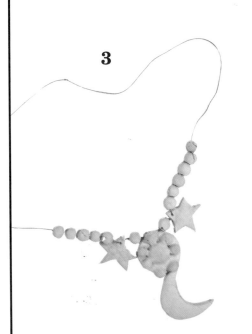

1. You can make use of a reaction which involves heat to make your own jewelry. To begin with, make a thick dough with flour and water. Knead well to get rid of any air bubbles in the dough.

2. Shape the dough to give you beads and pendants like the ones you can see in the picture. You can also try your own designs – if they go wrong simply squash them up and start again!

2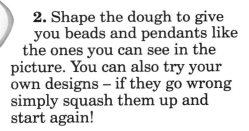

3

3. It is best to work on a lightly floured surface and to rub a little flour onto your hands too. This will stop the dough from sticking. If the dough is too sticky, sprinkle it with flour and knead it for a little longer.

4. Before baking, leave each shape to harden and pierce with a skewer to give a hole. With the help of an adult, bake in the oven on a medium heat until hard. Allow to cool, paint and varnish. When dry, thread the shapes onto a necklace!

4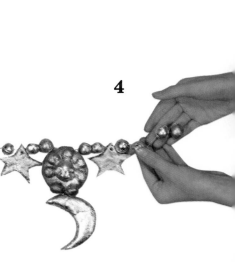

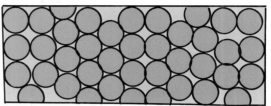
Water evaporates when the dough is baked

WHY IT WORKS

When flour is mixed with water, it forms a dough as the flour molecules are suspended in the liquid (1). A sticky substance called gluten is also formed and the dough can be molded into all sorts of shapes. When the dough is baked in the oven, the water evaporates leaving behind the flour molecules which form a solid mass (2).

1

2

BRIGHT IDEAS

You could try changing the ingredients to get better doughs. Add a little oil and/or cream of tartare to your dough to make it more pliable.

If you enjoy this project, you could buy some specialist modeling clay and create more personalized jewelry using your own designs.

Heat And Change

When a substance is heated, several things might happen to it. It may appear not to change (apart from the fact that it is hotter); for example, common salt which is dry and pure may change, but returns to its original state as it cools. Some substances can change permanently. Look at the burnt toast on the left – this is an example of a permanent change. When a permanent change takes place there could be a change in appearance or smell, like the toast; gases and smoke could be given off and sounds could be made, like the crackling of burning wood. There could also be changes in weight, volume or color. As you carry out this next project make a note of any changes that take place.

Uncover The Secret

1. In the past, invisible inks were used to write secret information. Onion juice and milk were often used, but we will be using lemon juice. Begin by squeezing the juice from a lemon into a jar.

2. To give your message a really original look, find a feather and trim the end to provide a quill to write with. Give your paper an ancient look by leaving it in a warm oven (which is turned OFF) until it turns light brown. Don't leave it too long or it may burn!

3. Write your message in large, clear writing. As soon as the lemon juice is dry, it will look as if the page is blank. Next, you will need the help of an adult.

WHY IT WORKS

When the lemon juice is heated, the water molecules are evaporated away and the remaining compounds combine with the oxygen in the air. This is known as oxidization and the result is that the lemon juice turns brown. Compare this with the effect of scorching a cotton shirt with an iron. The fabric of the shirt turns brown because of oxidization.

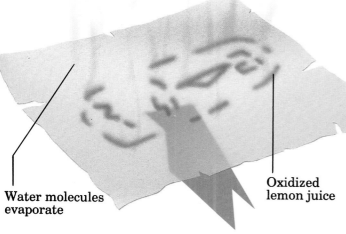

Water molecules evaporate

Oxidized lemon juice

BRIGHT IDEAS

To make honeycomb toffee, put two cups (1lb) sugar, one and a quarter cups of water (10oz) and four tablespoons of vinegar into a large pan. Stir and slowly bring to the boil until the mixture reaches 280°F. Remove from heat and add half a teaspoon of bicarbonate of soda and stir. Pour into a buttered tin and leave to set. Never taste toffee until it has cooled down!

4. Heat the paper up. If you use a candle, you MUST keep the paper moving or it may catch fire. Alternatively, you could iron the paper or put it in a warm oven for a minute. The effect should be the same, the heat makes the secret message appear!

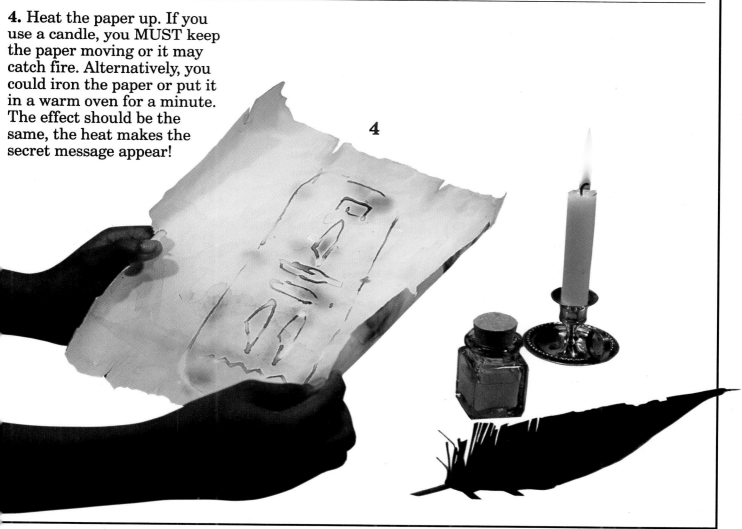

4

DIFFERENT REACTIONS

If you squeeze the juice from an orange or eat a slice of fresh lemon, you will find that they taste quite sour. This is because they contain acids. An alkali is the opposite of an acid. Medicines such as milk of magnesia are alkaline, and are used to cure pains caused by too much acid in the stomach. It combines with the acid and produces a mixture which is not acidic or alkaline, but neutral. Farmers use lime to neutralize the acids in soil in a similar way. On the left you can see an "electronic pH detector", this would be used by a scientist to show how acidic or alkaline a solution is.

BRIGHT IDEAS

You could try making other indicators. Blackberries, blueberries and beetroot all give a strong dye. Make sheets of indicator paper just as you did for the project.

Make solutions by dissolving different substances in a little water and then test them. Do the same kind of color changes take place? Some things to try are: sucking candies, sugar, salt, lemonade, toothpaste, fresh milk, sour milk and anteacid tablets.

COLOR INDICATOR

1

1. To make your own pH detector, ask an adult to help you with the first two steps of this project. Cut a fresh red cabbage into small pieces.

3

2. Place the cabbage in a pan and cover with water. Bring to a boil and simmer for about 10 minutes. Remove from the heat and then leave to stand for 1 hour.

2

3. Strain the juice and throw away the cabbage (or you can eat it). Now, dip sheets of blotting paper into the juice and then leave them to dry. This is your indicator paper.

4. Collect different inks to write on the paper. Acidic inks include sour milk, lemon juice and vinegar. Alkaline inks are fresh milk and washing soda dissolved in water.

4

WHY IT WORKS

Acids and alkalis produce chemical reactions when they mix with other things. In their reactions with indicators they cause color changes. The purple dye from the cabbage turns red in acids and green in alkalis. It is possible to tell from an indicator how strong an acid or an alkali is. This strength is measured on the pH scale.

On the pH scale, number 1, the red color on the right, is a strong acid. Number 7, yellow in the centre, is neutral. Number 14, blue on the left, is a strong alkali.

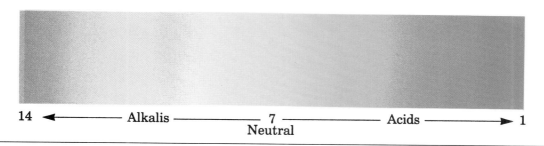

14 ◀—————— Alkalis —————— 7 ————— Acids —————▶ 1
Neutral

5

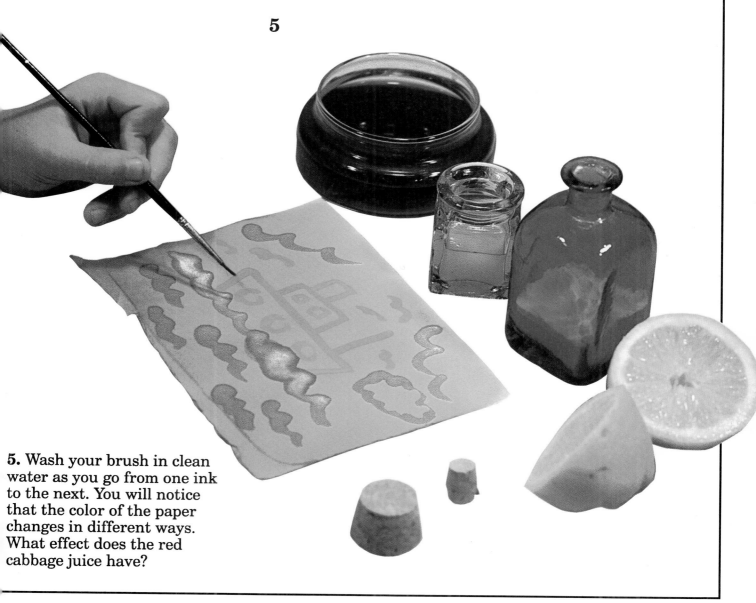

5. Wash your brush in clean water as you go from one ink to the next. You will notice that the color of the paper changes in different ways. What effect does the red cabbage juice have?

INVISIBLE REACTIONS

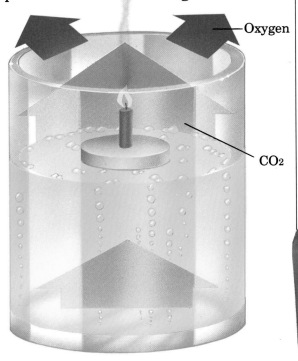

Already in this book, we have seen how ice melting, baking powder fizzing, toast burning and even washing your hands involve reactions and changes. Did you realize, though, that when a fire is burning, a chemical reaction is taking place, and to stop a fire we have to stop the chemical reaction? There are many ways of stopping a fire; we can use fire extinguishers, buckets of sand, water, foam or wet blankets. In this project, we will see how one reaction which you have produced already can be used to fight a fire.

WHY IT WORKS

When you light the candle, you start a reaction between the wick of the candle (which is full of wax – the fuel of the fire) and the oxygen in the air. The heat of the candle burning keeps the reaction between the fuel and the oxygen going. The reaction between the lemon juice and the baking powder produces carbon dioxide (CO_2). CO_2 is heavier than the air in the jar so the air is pushed up and out of the jar by the CO_2. Without the oxygen in the air, the burning reaction stops and the flame is extinguished.

4. The fizzing should carry on for a few minutes. If it does not, add more baking powder and lemon juice.

4

Oxygen

CO₂

BRIGHT IDEAS

💡 A good scientist would ask questions about a test like this. Was it really the carbon dioxide which put the flame out? Perhaps the oxygen in the jar was all used up anyway? Or maybe a draft put the flame out? To see whether the reaction between the lemon juice and the baking powder really did make a difference, we need to set up a control. Repeat the test in the project, but this time have two identical jars with candles burning in them. Do not add anything to the second jar after the candle has been lit. This jar is known as the control. Compare what happens as you follow the project with the first jar. If the candle in the control jar burns for longer, you have proved that the CO_2 produced in the project did make a difference!

5. The flame of the candle will dim and then die completely. At this point, you could repeat the experiment to see if this always happens.

5

FIRE EXTINGUISHER

1. You'll need the soap boat that you made on page 12. Remove the mast and fix a small candle in its place. Float the candle in a little water at the bottom of a deep jar. Light it with a spill.

1

2. Add several spoons of baking powder to the water and stir the mixture gently with a long spatula.

2

3. Before the baking powder and the water stop fizzing, add a good measure of lemon juice. Watch closely to see what happens.

3

25

ELECTRICITY & REACTIONS

About 200 years ago, an Italian called Alessandro Volta produced a current of electricity with layers of zinc and silver separated by cardboard soaked in salt water. Later, two Englishmen, William Nicholson and Anthony Carlisle, connected the terminals of the pile to metal rods and placed the rods in water. Bubbles of gas were given off by the rods; oxygen on the positive rod and hydrogen on the negative rod – the two gases which make water! This led to the development of electroplating (left), the process of coating one metal with another metal, for example, iron is coated with zinc to prevent rusting.

SEPARATING WATER

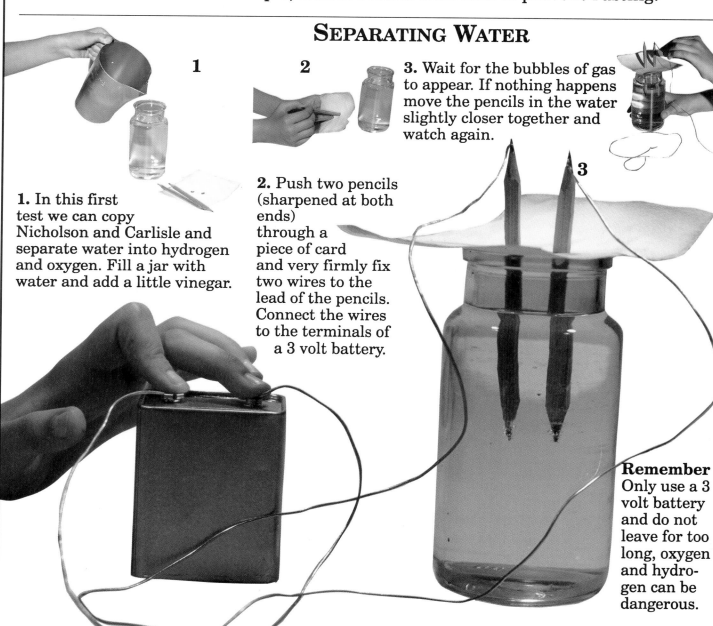

1. In this first test we can copy Nicholson and Carlisle and separate water into hydrogen and oxygen. Fill a jar with water and add a little vinegar.

2. Push two pencils (sharpened at both ends) through a piece of card and very firmly fix two wires to the lead of the pencils. Connect the wires to the terminals of a 3 volt battery.

3. Wait for the bubbles of gas to appear. If nothing happens move the pencils in the water slightly closer together and watch again.

Remember Only use a 3 volt battery and do not leave for too long, oxygen and hydrogen can be dangerous.

WHY IT WORKS

In the first project, the electrical current passes from the positive terminal, through the solution, to the negative terminal. The flow of electricity causes a reaction in which the molecules of water, H_2O, are split up into atoms of oxygen and hydrogen. Oxygen is given off at the positive terminal and hydrogen at the negative. In electroplating (right), the electrical current releases particles of the metal on the positive terminal, in this case copper, and they move to the negative side coating the silver coin.

BRIGHT IDEAS

A common reaction of a metal with water is the conversion of iron to rust. Try to prevent rust by putting a nail in a jar of water (1) with another nail coated in a substance that keeps out air and water, for example, grease (2). What happens to the nails after a few days?

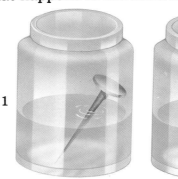

ELECTROPLATING

1

1. This project allows you to see electroplating in action. Make 2 small holes in the lid of a jar and fix 2 short pieces of plastic straw into them.

2

2. Thread two wires through the straws. Connect a paper clip to the end of each wire and attach a copper coin and a silver coin.

3

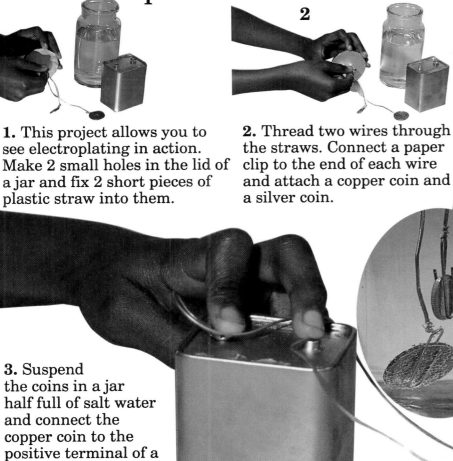

3. Suspend the coins in a jar half full of salt water and connect the copper coin to the positive terminal of a 3 volt battery and the silver coin to the negative. The silver coin will slowly take on a copper color.

ORGANIC REACTIONS

One set of reactions which we have not talked about yet are those where living things change compounds or elements into new compounds. These are called organic reactions and the most common are the ones caused by tiny creatures called micro-organisms. These include bacteria and molds. Most molds are unpleasant and unhelpful to us. One very useful mold, however, is yeast. It acts on the ingredients used in making beer (left), turning the sugar to alcohol and when mixed into the bread dough, it makes it rise. Louis Pasteur was a scientist who discovered many things about micro-organisms. In particular, he found out how harmful organisms in food could be killed off by heating, the process now known as pasteurization.

RAISING DOUGH

1. To make your own bread, mix two tablespoons of dried yeast with one teaspoon of sugar and one cup of warm (not hot) water. Leave until frothy.

2. Mix 5 cups of wholemeal flour, 2 tbs of caster sugar, 4tsp of salt and 1oz of shortening in a bowl. Stir in the yeast mixture and 2.5 cups of tepid water.

3. Remove from the bowl and knead the dough on a floured board until it becomes firm and elastic but not sticky. Don't rush this bit!

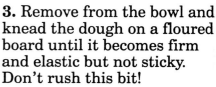

3

1

2

7. Ask an adult to help you now. Heat up the oven to 450°. Remove the clear plastic wrap and bake your bread in the oven for 30 to 40 minutes.

8. When you think your bread is cooked, remove it from the oven. Push a skewer into the bread; if it is still sticky inside it needs longer in the oven.

9. When the bread is cooked, remove it from the baking trays and place on a wire rack to cool. Fresh bread is delicious when still warm.

WHY IT WORKS

The reaction of yeast with sugar is an organic example of a chemical change which is speeded up by the heat from the warm water. Sugar is a compound made of carbon, hydrogen and oxygen. Substances in the yeast called enzymes turn the sugar into alcohol and also produce large amounts of carbon dioxide gas. The gas bubbles are what make the bread rise.

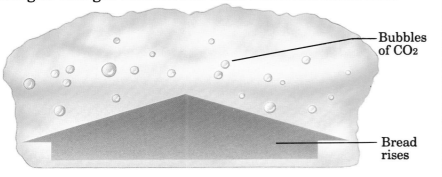

Bubbles of CO_2

Bread rises

BRIGHT IDEAS

To make some butter for your bread, put one cup of cream into a clean jar. Screw the lid on tightly and shake the jar for a long time. Eventually the cream separates and turns into a solid, butter, and a liquid, buttermilk. Remove the butter by straining through a sieve. Add a little salt to the butter and then beat it with a fork until it is smooth. Spread it on your freshly-baked bread and enjoy it!

4. Leave the dough in a lightly oiled bowl in a warm place. Cover the bowl with clear plastic wrap to keep the moisture in.

5. When the dough has risen, put it on a floured surface and knead until firm.

6. Place on lightly oiled baking trays, brush with salty water, sprinkle with a little flour, cover with clear plaastic wrap and leave to rise once more.

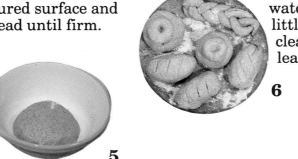

6

4

5

REACTIONS WITH LIGHT

This final reaction is perhaps the most important one of all. It is called photosynthesis and is the process by which green plants use the energy from sunlight to help in the production of food such as sugars. Why is this so important? The cells in the bodies of animals, including human beings, are not capable of producing these basic foods. Therefore, they have to eat plants or other animals to stay alive. If the Sun did not shine and photosynthesis stopped, life would die out as the planet's food stores were used up.

BRIGHT IDEAS

The experiment with the cellophane shows how you can speed up reactions with light to create shapes. You can use photographic paper in a similar way. Get some photographic paper from a photographic supply store. Put it in a sunny, dry place with a few objects on it, for example, coins and bits of jewelry. After a few days, remove the objects and look at the effect. The paper will turn black where the light hits it, leaving white shapes where the objects were placed.

PLANT PATTERNS

1

1. To stop sunlight from reaching a plant's leaves, we can block it out with a small piece of aluminum foil. Cut out a sun-shape to stick on the leaf. Fix it to the leaf using flour and water.

2. Because you will probably have to leave your sun-shape on the plant for several days, it is a good idea to strengthen the foil. You can do this by sticking it onto some paper. Treat the plant normally and leave the shape in place for two weeks or more. During this time, you could experiment further by putting similar shapes on other plants around the house. Try comparing the different effects of the aluminum foil and black pen on cellophane (see stage 3) on the same plant.

2

WHY IT WORKS

Plants take their green color from a green pigment called chlorophyll. When the plant is exposed to sunlight, the chlorophyll absorbs the energy which then assists a reaction in the plant. The Sun also helps the plant to produce more green chlorophyll. Where the Sun is blocked out by the foil, a lighter patch develops. A waste product of photosynthesis is oxygen which the plants release into the air. Animals take oxygen from the air and breathe out carbon dioxide – just the reverse.

Sunlight

Aluminum foil blocks out sunlight

Lighter patch develops as less chlorophyll is produced

3

3. Plants respond not only to the amount of light they receive but also to the color of the light. This time, use a black pen to draw the sun-shape on a piece of cellophane. As sunlight passes through the shape it becomes blue light, leaving a darker shape underneath as more chlorophyll is produced.

31

Scientific Terms

ATOM The smallest part of any element.

BACTERIA Simple organisms which consist of only one cell and cause organic reactions.

COMPOUND A substance made up of two or more elements. It cannot be split up into its separate elements by a physical process.

ELECTROLYSIS Splitting up a liquid into its separate elements by passing an electric current through it.

ELECTROPLATING The process of putting a metallic coating on a metal by using an electric current.

ELEMENT A simple substance which is made up of only one kind of atom.

INDICATORS Substances which change color when they are put into contact with acids or alkalis.

MIXTURE A combination of elements and compounds which can be separated by a physical process.

MOLECULE The smallest part of a compound that can exist on its own.

pH SCALE A scale which measures the strength of acids and alkalis where 1 is a strong acid, 7 is neutral and 14 is a strong alkali.

REACTION A process where two substances combine to form a new substance (or substances).

SOLUTION A liquid into which a substance, solid or gas, has been dissolved.

Index